Mindset for Healing

REVIEWS / RECOMMENDATIONS

I have had the pleasure of treating Tirtzah both pre and post cancer diagnosis. As a Certified Health and Wellness Coach, Tirtzah had a wide array of tools to implement in her own treatment plan. These tools allowed her body and mind to heal. She has taken her experiences and shared in a wonderful, easy to read book, "Mindset for Healing". The book offers the reader insight on ways they may help themselves and is a wonderful resource for all to read. I highly recommend it for anyone going through any type of healing journey be it physical, emotional or spiritual.

Dr. Shauna Hindman

When something unexpected comes along that turns your world upside down, it can cause a flurry of racing thoughts, gripping fear and chaotic emotions. At a time like this...it's comforting to know that someone has paved the way and is now helping others...just like you! Mindset for Healing, A Profound Plan to See Healing from a New Perspective by Tirtzah Sandor, while written because of her journey through a physical illness, her story and "new perspective" is equally beneficial for any other type of healing that is needed; healing from a broken relationship, healing from emotional wounds or healing from a mindset of belief systems that are no longer serving you.

Mindy J. Kaleta
Ladybug Junction Farm
www.mindyjkaleta.com

Mindset for Healing

A Profound Yet Simple Plan to See Healing from a New Perspective

TIRTZAH SANDOR

Published by Healing Hamsa Publishing and Media

ISBN–13: 978-1-7323697-0-2

DISCLAIMER

The author does not dispense medical advice, nor prescribe any treatment. This book is advice for healthcare and needs to be used as a *supplement* to working with doctors or other trained professionals. The author's intent is to help you in your quest for creating a mindset for healing to create a way for you to heal in mind, body and spirit. You are choosing to use this book to help move you forward on your healing journey. The publisher and author disclaim liability for any of your actions.

Although the author and publisher have endeavored to ensure that the information provided herein is complete and accurate, they shall not be held responsible for loss or damage of any nature suffered as a result of reliance on any of this book's contents or any errors or omissions herein.

GRATITUDE

There are so many people to thank that supported me and encouraged me to write this book. First, I want to thank all the friends and family who read my Caringbridge.com posts weekly and encouraged me to share my journey, which took a slight detour in this book. That will be my next book. A huge thank you to all the healers along my journey that enhanced the healing process. Special thanks to the core of my healing team: Nick Ciranni, massage therapist extraordinaire; Dr. Shauna Hindman, chiropractor and acupuncturist; and Dr. Doug Maxeiner, chiropractor. A special thank you to my surgical oncologist, Kristine Slam, M.D. and my medical oncologist, Jeanna Knoble, M.D. who were willing to work with me to release the cancer. Thanks to Dr. Hari Sharma, Ayurveda Practitioner at Ohio State University. A huge thank you to my wonderful friend Chris Starkey for editing. Jodi Krizer Graber—there are not enough words to thank you for all the encouragement, weekly meetings, support and especially your friendship. Dr. Ellen Pill for your friendship, willingness to help out when needed and interviewing me to write the bio and information for the cover, about the book and about me. Tara Meyer–Robson at Happy Peacock Publishing and author of The Flow Method for writing the foreword and for all the help and support in publishing this book. I could not have done this without you! To DLD Books for their help in formatting and uploading. To the wonderful congregation of Temple Beth Shalom in New Albany, OH. Thanks Dad for your support. To my daughter Manette, I love you bunches. Last but definitely not least, a huge thank you to my wonderful husband Rick who has always supported me, even when he thought I was a little bonkers. Thank you, thank you, thank you.

DEDICATION

This book is dedicated to all the people willing to choose to take control of their own healing journey by empowering themselves to change their perspective about healing and take the steps to create a mindset for healing.

FOREWORD

When faced with a serious diagnosis, where do you turn? How do you create an empowered healing plan? How do you find hope in a difficult time, and how do you keep that hope going through treatments and side effects?

If you are like so many faced with this dilemma, you've likely researched methods, books, the latest science, and more about whatever dis–ease you are dealing with. If you've done this, then you will know that it seems as if there are as many books on the healing process as there are diseases. Look deeper and you'll find that, more often than not, the best ones are penned by people courageous and aware enough to share their real journeys through the healing process and to document the way they got there. This is such a program.

In 2016, Tirtzah Sandor was diagnosed with triple–negative, stage 3 breast cancer, a daunting diagnosis by anyone's standards. However, instead of giving in to fear and giving up her power to the diagnosis, she used it as a way to learn about herself, her strength, and the power of positivity. More than that, she fully embraced the journey of self–empowerment and used this diagnosis as an opportunity to be more fully authentic and more fully present than ever. In so doing, she created a 10–step process to help her to heal, and now shares that process with you.

In following this program, you will feel that Tirtzah is right there next to you as a trusted guide, gently walking you through the vital steps she took to release cancer from her body. Fully aware of the power of words, she shows you why it's so vital to choose the words you use in the process of healing, as words have power. For instance, while most of us have been conditioned to think of healing from a disease as serious as cancer as a fight and are heralded as a "warrior" in the process of going through treatments, she rightly notes that when we use these kinds of war references in our process for healing, we are really declaring war against ourselves. Instead, she advocates for a focus on "releasing" the disease from the body, and her 10–step process will help you to do just that.

Even better, this process can be used for any kind of healing, whether it is from a physical disease, a difficult loss, or any other kind of stress or problem you might be facing. In this way, *Mindset for Healing* is accessible and useful to all people, and most especially to anyone going through a challenging time.

Throughout the program, Tirtzah gently invites you to question authority and opinions in a healthy way, and then to make decisions about your healing that align with what you truly believe is the right decision. In my experience, this step is critical to any person setting out on a healing journey, and yet it is one not frequently encouraged. There can be almost no more important decision when faced with a health crisis than selecting your healing team and treatment plan, but far too many people are intimidated by asking questions or requesting a second opinion. Tirtzah not only encourages you to seek the right answers for you, but she shows you precisely why this is such a critical part of releasing dis–ease.

In all, she has created a beautiful healing process that will enable you to feel supported, loved, and understood as you create your own path to wellbeing and create your own "mindset for healing." More than just a mindset, what Tirtzah encourages you to do is to create a fully conscious, empowered life that will see you through the dis–ease and allow you to come out the other side with more strength, awareness, and sense of self than when you started.

Tara Meyer–Robson
Author, *The Flow Method: 40 Days to Total Life Transformation*
www.TaraMeyerRobson.com

Table of Contents

Introduction

> *"Healing takes courage, and we all have courage, even if we have to dig a little to find it."*
> ***Tori Amos***

> *"If you really want to heal and move forward in your life, make time to create a new mindset and a new perspective on how to heal."*
> ***Tirtzah Sandor***

This book came about as I was in the process of writing about my journey to release triple negative, inflammatory, stage three breast cancer. As I began writing, I realized the most important thing I did to help myself heal was to use a "mindset for healing." I believe this mindset was a strong part of why I was able to release the cancer in 2016, work through two major knee surgeries, and heal from "sick building syndrome" many years ago. "The **sick building syndrome** (SBS) is used to describe a situation in which the occupants of a **building** experience acute health– or comfort–related effects that seem to be linked directly to the time spent in the **building**. No specific illness or cause can be identified."[1]

Healing Note

*Disease literally means "lack of ease."
Hyphenating the word brings focus to being in a
natural state of ease. I have chosen to use the
hyphenated dis–ease in this book so your focus is
shifted from the illness to the state of mind to
become more at ease.*

Even though I wrote this with the intention that my main audience are those facing an illness, *Mindset for Healing* **is for everyone**. We all need healing of some sort at some point in our lives. By creating a mindset for healing, you are changing how you think and speak about whatever it is you need to overcome (e.g. negative thoughts, illness, getting stuck, your life outlook). This mindset was so important during my healing journey to release breast cancer. It allowed me to see the dis–ease for what it was and opened my heart and mind to realizing what I needed to do, say, and think to release the stuck energy in me. Not only do ***you*** need to create a mindset for healing for yourself, I suggest you ask everyone around you to do the same. Share this attitude with friends and family and ask them to send only positive thoughts and energy, and to speak of healing in positive ways to create the best healing environment for you.

My mindset for healing allowed me to move through

the journey to release cancer and kept me in a positive frame of mind. I kept a journal that I posted on Caringbridge.com (see more about this later in the book). Quite a few people who were reading my online journal and others I was speaking with encouraged me to share this mindset and the way I handled the journey to release the cancer and continue to heal my mind, body and spirit.

People I met that embraced this mindset were the ones that made the most progress with whatever challenge they were facing. My husband would take me to chemotherapy and each time he noticed people who were told that they could not get a treatment that day. Either something in their blood draw was off, or they were not feeling well. These patients, for the most part, appeared to have a defeatist attitude and looked as though they were not taking care of themselves. Some visibly appeared to have given up. I understand that facing a diagnosis of cancer or any dis–ease is a challenge, yet it was so very sad to see. **It is how you face the challenge that matters!**

One of the other healing journeys in my life was in 1988 when I had my second knee surgery. Since they moved my knee cap and clipped and reattached the quadricep in my knee for the second time, the quadricep decided it didn't want to activate or fire for some time; the muscle had atrophied and would not work properly. At one of my physical therapy appointments, I overheard the physical therapist on the phone with my doctor saying they were not sure I would walk again. I chose not to believe this statement. I adopted the attitude that I **was** going to walk again and did everything in my power to make it happen. Today, even though I am still bone on bone and have been since the operation, I not only walk, but I have almost full range of motion. During this journey, I found out I had a lot more inner strength than I ever realized. This is one thing you may discover from reading and doing the exercises I have put forth in this book.

> *"Life's challenges are not supposed to paralyze you, they're supposed to help you discover who you are."*
> **Bernice Johnson Reagon**

About the Book

I have made the plan as easy and doable as possible so that you can take your time and move through the journey in a calm and simple manner.

Each chapter describes a step, how you benefit from it and then includes easy no or low–cost exercises to help you move through the step. Each chapter contains a Healing Note with additional information and quotes to inspire you along the way.

At the end of the book, there is a resource page for articles, websites and book suggestions and you can find more information on my website:
www.mindsetforhealing.com or www.tirtzahsandor.com.

I am a firm believer that when it is your time, you are going to pass no matter what you do. However, since we don't know for sure when it *is* our time, why not make the most of your healing to live life to its fullest?

You picked up this book because you are in pain and/or need healing of some sort and it reached out to you. Or, perhaps you saw this book and wanted it to support a friend or family member in need of healing. This means that creating the mindset for healing is ***something you want to do***, not think you should or have been told you have to do this. I applaud you for following your intuition and taking this important step of being your own ***advocate on your healing journey*** or being open to support someone you care about.

In the United States we have been conditioned to follow allopathic medicine (mainstream or Western medicine) and are sometimes told that alternative or complementary medicine[2] is bunk, voodoo, etc.

It is becoming more common to combine the allopathic treatments with alternative/complementary healing modalities. Many studies have been and are being conducted to prove that positive mindset, belief, mindfulness, acupuncture, energy healing, prayer, etc. really do make a difference. (See the resource page for links to studies not noted in this book.)

At the time this book was written, most insurance companies cover only allopathic (western) medical treatments. Hopefully that will change with more scientific research showing the benefits of alternative/complementary treatments.

I personally did more alternative and complementary medicine and believe I was able to release the cancer much more quickly than if I had done only allopathic medicine. I did discuss all of my treatments with my medical team so they were aware of everything I was doing to release my cancer.

Notice I said "RELEASE THE CANCER." Not battle, fight, be a warrior, etc.

Here are the definitions for these words according to Dictionary.com:

Battle

1. A hostile encounter or engagement between opposing military forces: *the battle of Waterloo.*
2. Participation in such hostile encounters or engagements: *wounds received in battle.*
3. A fight between two persons or animals: *ordering a trial by battle to settle the dispute.*
4. Any conflict or struggle: *a battle for control of the Senate.*
5. Archaic: *a battalion.*

(Note: Notice lots of hostility in the definitions above)

Fight

1. A battle or combat.
2. Any contest or struggle: *a fight for recovery from an illness.*

   (Note: Interesting that this is used as a definition for fight in the dictionary. No wonder we are

conditioned to use this word!)

3. An angry argument or disagreement: *whenever we discuss politics, we end up in a fight.*
4. Boxing: *a bout or contest.*
5. A game or diversion in which the participants hit or pelt each other with something harmless: *a pillow fight; a water fight.*
6. Ability, will, or inclination to fight: *there was no fight left in him.*

(Note: Lots of anger and aggression in these definitions.)

Warrior

1. A person engaged or experienced in warfare; soldier.
2. A person who shows or has shown great vigor, courage, or aggressiveness, as in politics or athletics.

Conquered

To gain or acquire by force of arms: *conquer territory*

1. To overcome by force of arms: *conquered the enemy*
2. To gain mastery over or win by overcoming obstacles or opposition: conquered the mountain
3. To overcome by mental or moral power: *conquered her fear*
4. To be victorious [3]

(Note: The first two definitions are fairly negative, the last 2 are more positive. These would be better words to use in my opinion.)

All of these words have very negative connotations. The question then becomes what are you battling, fighting, being a warrior against and trying to conquer? Where are you directing your anger and hostility? Most people will answer the cancer or the dis-ease.

Where is the cancer or dis-ease located? Isn't it in your body? This means you are fighting, battling, being a warrior against, conquering, being angry at, or hostile toward YOURSELF!

By doing this, you create negativity in your mind, body and spirit. Wouldn't it be better to choose to find ways to work with your mind, body, and spirit instead of working against yourself?

Ask yourself: How does this negative frame of mind help me to release –– which means set free or escape from confinement–– the dis-ease or help me to heal? Write down the answers that come to you and take a good look at what you wrote. Then decide if you are ready to make changes to begin to help yourself.

I spent a lot of time going over the order of the steps and decided on this arrangement for the following reasons.

Before you can create a *mindset for healing*, you have to **CHOOSE** to make a change or changes. Once you have made the choice, you have to choose to **BE YOU** and not allow the dis-ease or anything or anyone else to change this. Then you have to **BELIEVE** the choices you are making are the *right ones for you*. To do this, **SELF–CARE** allows you to make changes and create a mindset for healing. Next, you need to **EMPOWER** yourself to make the tough choices and decide the **DIRECTION** you want your healing journey to take. To make this all happen, you need to add **POSITIVITY** to your life and find ways to add **FORGIVENESS** for yourself and others. Once you have taken the previous steps you are ready to find paths of **ENJOYMENT** and find ways to **LIVE** the life you want using the *mindset for healing* to get you there.

A good way to get some input on how your healing journey *may go* is to ask others about their journey and what it was like for them. Ask them about the emotions they went through, which treatments worked for them, references for potential doctors, anything you can think of. Take their information and choose how or if you will incorporate it into *your* healing journey. Remember, each person heals differently and in their own time. Be careful not to "*compare and despair*" because someone's healing journey took less time or went in a different direction than yours. Each person will have different symptoms and reactions depending on their body. Give yourself time to heal the way YOUR body needs to heal.

Since each of us is unique and has our own path to follow, I encourage you do the steps at your own pace. Choose wisely for **YOU!**

When you complete part of your personal healing plan (a treatment for any dis-ease you are working on releasing, steps you are taking to heal in mind or spirit, completing a step in this plan, or even noticing a positive change) be sure to **CELEBRATE!** This can be a small celebration or something big. One of the things I did during my healing journey from the breast cancer diagnosis was to celebrate each step of the journey (end of first chemo, end of second chemo, great blood test results, feeling good for a day, etc). Some of my celebrations were small like doing a happy dance, some were going out and buying something I had always wanted, others were making the time and effort to share the moment with friends.

My biggest celebration was close to the end of the medical portion of the healing journey. I chose to change my name from Geri Sue to Tirtzah. I did this because I did not feel like I was the same person at the end of my journey; I had changed in so many ways.

The name Tirtzah was given to me many years ago at camp when I was 16 or so by a friend and no one ever called me by this name but this one friend during the one summer. When I started thinking about a new name, Tirtzah came back to me even though I hadn't thought of it for years. I looked up the definition and it means, hope, delight, desire. After I had chosen the name, I learned that in the Bible, Tirtzah was an outspoken female who represented her family to Moses and was able to get changes made in the law so they could inherit land. Everything about the name resonated with me, so now I am known as Tirtzah and proud of it.

On my birthday, I went through two Jewish ceremonies to take on the new name, including going to the Mikvah (Jewish ritual bath) and had a naming ceremony at our temple at Friday night services. I worked with the Rabbis and wrote my own ceremonies for each so it was very personal and spiritual. This experience was and continues to be extremely empowering. Taking on a new identity was a very important way to acknowledge not only to me, but to the world that I have changed and am now a different person in so many ways. By doing this on my birthday, it felt like a true rebirth.

I invite you to create your own ceremony around each celebration. At the end of the book, I have a section on celebrations. See if any work for you. Use the suggested celebrations as stated, change them in any way that is meaningful to you, or create your own unique celebrations.

This is my invitation to you to join me in creating a *mindset for healing*. I invite you to read all the steps, then choose to follow them in the sequence I set forth or do them in an order that feels right for *you*.

ARE YOU READY TO MAKE A PERSONAL COMMITMENT TO HELP YOURSELF HEAL?

> *"Please keep in mind the distinction between healing and treatment: treatment originates from outside, whereas healing comes from within."*
> **Andrew Weil MD**

Dis–ease can potentially be stuck energy that needs to be released.

Albert Einstein said, "Everything is energy and that's all there is to it. Match the frequency of the reality you want and you cannot help but get that reality. It can be no other way. This is not philosophy. This is physics."

In *Anatomy of the Spirit, The Seven Stages of Power and Healing,* Caroline Myss states the following about energy and healing,

"Our emotions reside physically in our bodies and interact with our cells and tissues, in fact Dr. Candace Pert[4] can no longer separate the mind from the body, she says, because the same kinds of cells that manufacture and receive emotional chemistry in the brain are present throughout the body."

Taking time to connect with your emotions and finding ways to understand and deal with them is a great way to help you release stuck energy.

An article in the August 2017 Psychology Today magazine entitled *"When Healing is a No–Brainer"* by Samuel Veissie´re speaks about how the brain can be tricked into healing using suggestion–assisted healing techniques. It states, *"The healing potential of culturally enhanced suggestion may become the no–brainer treatment choice for many conditions that resist standard medical care."*

> *"Nothing in life is solid. It may look solid, it may even feel solid, but it is not. It is all energy and energy can be moved, molded and changed at will."*
> **Tara Meyer–Robson from The Flow Method**

Now that you better understand what this book it all about, it is:

TIME TO BEGIN!!

CREATE A MINDSET FOR HEALING TO EMPOWER YOURSELF TO SEE HEALING FROM A NEW PERSPECTIVE

> *"You can't make positive choices for the rest of your life without an environment that makes those choices easy, natural, and enjoyable."*
> **Deepak Chopra**

> *"The soul always knows what to do to heal itself. The challenge is to silence the mind."*
> **Caroline Myss**

Create the calming environment you need to help you move through this experience. Find a quiet space; a space just for this, a space with no distractions. Have pen and paper or a special journal or notebook on hand for notes, light candles if you like, take a deep breath, do a quick meditation, open your mind, and begin reading.

Healing Note

Read through all the steps I've outlined. Then, decide if you will do them in the order given (my recommendation) or if a particular step is calling to you to start there or to do a little on each step. My recommendation is to take time to work with each step until you feel ready to move on. Do this at your own pace. And no matter how you choose to create your mindset for healing journey, know it is the right path for YOU!

Decide if you want to share your journey with family and friends. Sharing your journey is a great way to get support and help. You can do this privately or you can do this publicly. There are many websites for this purpose, such as Caringbridge.org.

Caringbridge was the best for me, but Posthope, carepages, and lotsahelpinghands are similar; while giveforward is more about fundraising; there are likely to be more along the same lines by now. Explore for the best one for you to reach friends and family, share your journey, ask for help, etc. (also see the resource page for link addresses).

Using one of the above websites allows you to share with only the people you choose instead of sharing publicly. You can also share on Facebook or other social media sites you are comfortable with; just remember these are all somewhat public spaces.

I particularly invite you to set an intention before you begin this "Mindset for Healing" journey so you are able to measure your success. Make this a simple intention such as: "I have created a healing mindset," or "I am healed," "I have released my dis–ease." I suggest you do an overall intention for the journey and then set a small intention for each section. You may want to set an intention daily or for each small step you want take. Write these intentions down. Write them in the present as if they have already happened. This makes them more powerful!

Be gentle with yourself as you go through this process. There may be events that you remember that cause you pain or there may be thoughts you would rather not deal with at the moment. (Some things that come up may require help from a professional. If this happens, I encourage you to contact someone.) Write down whatever comes to you and you can revisit it at a later time or sit with it and see why it came to you and how you can work through it.

Next, skim through all the chapters. You may want to read the Healing Notes and quotes the first time through. Then go back and read everything.

Read each chapter and go through the exercises until you feel are ready to move to the next one.

STEP ONE: CHOOSE!

Choose to heal not only the body, but also the mind and spirit

> *"One's philosophy is not best expressed in words; it is expressed in the choices one makes... and the choices we make are ultimately our responsibility."*
> **Eleanor Roosevelt**

Life is all about choices: what you choose to believe, what you choose to perceive, how you choose to react, how you choose to live, and the environment in which you choose to live. These choices shape your life.

The first step to creating a mindset for healing is to **choose to heal** and change your mindset to one that benefits **your** healing process. When you make this positive choice, miracles can happen. I have seen it in others and it happened to me.

I won't lie: **choosing and taking this path will be challenging and there will be setbacks.** How you handle the setbacks will make a difference in how you move forward. If you give yourself permission to sit and do nothing on the days you **really need to** (i.e., give yourself permission to have a day off or be angry for a short period of time, then move forward), you **will** heal faster. Allowing yourself to honor your feelings (without wallowing too long) is critical. If you allow yourself to stay in the negative mindset too long, however, you create more issues for yourself and may end up reversing your decision to heal. You can unintentionally reinforce the negative and may not heal as quickly or as well. I have faith in you and know you can do this! ***Believe in yourself!***

> *"If you so choose, even the unexpected setbacks can bring new and positive possibilities. If you so choose, you can find value and fulfillment in every circumstance."*
> **Ralph Marston**

Healing Note

View setbacks as a time to review and take stock of where you are, what you have learned, and to evaluate if you are going in the right direction. If you feel the direction is not right, change it. If you feel you are still going in the right direction, maybe you need to take it more slowly or re–do something you have already done to think of a new solution.

Choosing to heal means not only healing the body but healing the mind and spirit also. Healing just the body may be scratching the surface of what really needs to be healed. Some guidelines for body **and** mind are below; ways to heal the spirit follow.

Heal the Body

This is about taking the time to really care for your body. Making sure you are eating healthy, whole foods. Organic is best, when possible, because our bodies are not meant to digest the added chemicals in many non–organic fruits and vegetables.

Making time to exercise or do some movement.

Another thing to do to heal the body is make sure you are working with the right doctors; ones that will work with you and listen to your concerns and suggestions. Also, create a healing team of additional healers that you want in your life. (Mine is Team Tirtzah!). When I needed the right doctors and healers, I wrote in my journal about what I needed and wanted and asked the universe to provide them. Amazingly, at all the right times, the right people came into my life.

Get lots of rest! During a time of healing, your body requires more rest and more sleep. Make sure you get the six to eight hours of sleep your body needs and take time during the day to stop and rest.

Drink lots of water (see Healing Note in Step Four for how much to drink).

Step Four—Self–Care also covers healing the body in more detail.

Heal the Mind

Think positive thoughts. Make sure your thoughts are concentrated on the positive instead of the negative. Know that you will heal.

(Step Seven covers this is more detail.)

Practice mindfulness.

John Kabat Zinn states: "**Mindfulness** means paying attention in a particular way: on purpose, in the present moment, and nonjudgmentally." This can be done by practicing being in the present moment. Take 10 minutes to breathe and listen to what is going on inside you and around you. (See exercises below for more information on practicing mindfulness.)

Recall things you may have suppressed and find ways to release them (times when you held in/hang on to anger, resentment, hostility, etc). Write a question you have about past memories on a piece of paper or in your journal and meditate on it. Be open to listening and see what comes to you. Then write it down and take time to see what lessons came from the experience that have had a positive effect on your life.

Set the intention that everything will work. This again puts your mind into a more positive frame and allows the brain to set the body in motion to heal.

Find purpose in your life. What is it that you really want to do? What is your passion? What is your purpose? What is this healing journey teaching you? Journal what comes to mind when asking yourself these questions.

Take time to do all the exercises in this book.

Healing Note

*Spiritual healing is a very personal issue. I believe there is a difference between spirituality and religion. But, if you believe that religion **is** your spirituality then explore the ways you can pray and connect more fully with your beliefs and spirituality.*

Heal the Spirit

Take time to connect with your spirituality. Define what spirituality means to **you**. Then follow what you have set forth for yourself.

Read the books that call to you. Take time to expand your mind and read books on general spirituality or from other religions if you would like. (See the Resources Page for suggestions.)

Choose a spiritual goal for yourself during this journey and throughout your life.

EXERCISES

1. *Journal*

I have been journaling almost every day for seven years. I find it helpful in setting up my day, brain dumping (writing whatever comes into your brain so that you can stop thinking about it), and moving forward in the next direction I choose. I have also used journaling to ask questions and see what answers come to me while writing. I find this practice to be extremely empowering when you are willing to open up and allow thoughts to flow.

During my healing journey, there were times I journaled three to four times a day, and others whenever I needed it. You can use scraps of paper, your computer or a notebook. A gratitude journal or a regular journal, a dream journal, a thought journal or any combination of these will do. Here is an example of a combination journal. Exercise 2 is an example of a gratitude journal.

Journal Sheet

Date: _____

My Dreams:

_____

_____

_____

My Thoughts:

_____

_____

_____

My Intentions for Today:

_____

_____

_____

How I feel:

_____

_____

_____

Gratitude

_____

_____

_____

_____

Affirmations:

_____

_____

_____

Off to a:

_____

_____

_____

_____ day: (Example: Off to
a relaxing, fun, healing, abundant day filled with love and laughter.)

2. *Keep a Gratitude Journal*—A gratitude journal is best done at the end of the day. Write down three things you are grateful for and why.

3. Keep *a Gratitude Jar*—Write on slips of paper what or who you are grateful for and put the papers into a jar or container. At the end of the year, or whenever you are feeling ungrateful, for whatever reason, read what you have written.

4. *Send a Thank You Note*—Letting someone know you are grateful for them will not only make you feel better, you will brighten someone else's day.

5. *Practice Mindfulness*—Take a few moments to concentrate on your breath and just be in the present moment. Any time you begin to feel stressed, take three deep breaths before you move on.

6. *Meditate*—There is a plethora of information available about meditation and how it reduces stress, helps to center you, creates a way to help you deal with situations, and lowers your blood pressure. I make time to meditate at least once and often twice daily. During chemo, I used a specific meditation to help the chemo be directed only to the tumor. I used meditations to help let go, to help heal, and to connect with my higher

power. You can purchase CDs or download recordings. Also search YouTube for guided meditations (try searches like "healing meditations" or "letting go"). There are short and long ones, as well as spiritual meditations for whatever belief system you connect with. Do some research and find the people you connect with (note that the sound of their voice is very important) and begin a practice. (See other suggestions on the Resource Page.)

7. *Pray*—Whatever this means for you. You can pray while you meditate, pray in nature or pray at whatever religious building you choose. Taking a moment to be grateful and give thanks for everything good in your life may be a way of praying for you. Choose whatever works best for ***you***.

8. *Take a Walk in Nature*—This is another way to really connect to your spiritually. I find it amazing what nature has created for us! When I walk in the woods I feel connected to everything and find it to be very spiritual.

9. *Walk Barefoot in the Grass*—This is also known as grounding. It is a way to connect to the energy of the earth. If you live in an apartment or in the city where there may not be opportunities to find grass to ground in, you can purchase grounding

mats online (see the resource page for more information). You can also go to public parks, although you may want to be careful about going barefoot.

10. *Create a Healing Mantra*—One of the things that kept me going through my journey was a mantra I wrote. I would repeat it to myself daily and again whenever my spirit needed lifting. I would repeat it out loud if I could or silently in my head. Write your mantra in the present tense so you are sending the message that it is happening now. Write a mantra that works for you, or feel free to use mine:

   I am strong
   I am loved and supported
   I am healthy
   I am a thriver
   I am healed
   I am whole

STEP TWO:
BE YOU!

Choose to be you instead of the dis–ease—don't identify yourself as the dis–ease

> *"Dis–eases can be our spiritual flat tires—disruptions in our lives that seem to be disasters at the time but end by redirecting our lives in a meaningful way."*
> **Bernie Siegel**

When you say "I have cancer," "I have arthritis," "I have (*fill in the blank,*)" or "MY cancer," "MY arthritis," you are taking it on and **becoming it**. Instead, use words like "I was diagnosed with" or "I acknowledge that I have (fill in the blank)_____." Use the wording that resonates with you without claiming the dis–ease. Once you have chosen the words to use say: "I choose not to allow it to run my life."

Healing Note

The word "my" means belonging to. When you say "my dis–ease" you are saying the dis–ease belongs to you. When you view the dis–ease as something that does not belong to you, you can look at it more objectively and help yourself release it.

Accept that you have been diagnosed. This does not mean that you are the dis–ease. In the April 2017 AARP magazine, Michael J. Fox spoke of how he accepted and acknowledged the Parkinson's he was diagnosed with, but he did not allow it to become his life.

Again, this is about mindset and perception. Do you see yourself as being ill or do you see yourself as healthy and in a temporary state of ill health? Do you choose to live in fear or do you see yourself living a full life even during treatment or recovery? Can you see the dis–ease sitting in your body or do you visualize yourself releasing it?

If you allow the dis–ease to take over and run your life, you become whatever dis–ease is in your body.

When I was diagnosed with triple negative, inflammatory, Stage 3 breast cancer, I accepted the diagnosis but did **not** buy into the notion that a cancer diagnosis is a death sentence. I was grateful my doctors did not either. I chose to work every day to release the cancer. During the healing journey, I went on four trips, three where I had to travel by plane and one by car. I chose to live my life during the entire journey and had the blessing of my doctors to do so. I flew two days after a port [5] was put in, during the chemo treatments, and three weeks after my surgery. I told myself that everything was going to be fine and that I would take care of myself and take naps or do whatever I had to do so I was able to enjoy. I chose to persist and was fortunate that I was able to release the cancer.

(See more in Step 3 about Believe.)

"If you choose to not deal with an issue,
then you give up your right of control over the issue
and it will select the path of least resistance."
Susan Del Gatto

EXERCISES

1. Look in the mirror into your own eyes and tell yourself daily "I love you," "You are beautiful," and "I believe in you." This can be a real challenge for many people and it takes practice. It will potentially change a deep–seated belief that you are not worthy of love…you are!

2. Write an affirmation about healing that resonates with you. Example: I am healed and I am whole.

3. Listen to some of the meditations you found in your exercise in Step One.

4. Read books about healing (see the Resource page for suggestions).

STEP THREE: BELIEVE!

Choose to believe in yourself and in your personal power to heal

> *"From the beginning, I believed that I would get well and release the cancer. I asked everyone to believe with me. I am here today because of this belief."*
> ***Tirtzah Sandor***

Science is discovering more and more that the power of belief plays a huge role in healing.

"Belief is natural. It comes partly from the way our minds are hardwired," says Tanya Luhrmann, an anthropologist at Stanford University who has dedicated much of her professional life to understanding people's interactions with God.

She says that belief–based healing requires not only a good story but also the effort of an active listener—one with the ability to make what is imagined feel real. When story and imagination sync, the results can be astounding. "Humans have the capacity to change their experience," she says. "These are skills, and we can learn them." [6]

Studies using the placebo effect also support the idea of healing belief; i.e. if someone believed they were taking medicine that was going to make them better, they became better *even though they had been given a sugar pill instead of the medication.*

The following two paragraphs are from the article in the Aug. 2017 Psychology Today article entitled "When Healing is a No-Brainer":

"In the popular imagination, placebos are pills that have no medicinal properties and work through the power of belief alone. Because people expect them to be medicine, and the priestly class of medicine is wrapped in a halo of prestige, expectations do the heavy lifting of healing. But placebos need not entail a pill. Sham surgeries with nothing more than an anesthesia procedure and a superficial cut–and–stitch ritual have been shown to be very effective in the treatment of pain.

"More research is being done on 'social mechanisms that regulate attention and the powers of mind over body.' Some of them are meditation hypnosis and placebo effects."

The next three paragraphs are from another article on this subject by Dr. Joseph Mercola.

"A number of studies have revealed that placebos can work just as well as potent drugs. Sham surgery has even been shown to produce results that are equal to actual surgery!"

"Indeed, mounting research suggests this 'power of the mind,' or power of belief, can be a very healing force. Studies into the placebo effect also show that many conventional treatments 'work' because of the placebo effect and little else.

"The idea that 'perception is everything' certainly appears to hold true when it comes to medical treatment, and this includes perceptions about quality and price. Oftentimes, the more expensive the drug is the more effective it is *believed* to be—even if there's no evidence to support such a belief." [7]

Most important of all, ***believe in yourself***.

I believed from the very beginning that I was going to be able to release my cancer. My wonderful editor, Chris Starkey, provided me with these notes as she was editing this book. "My father did this, too! He started his second round of cancer with the affirmation that he was going to "'kick cancer's ass'" and the whole family repeated it back to him every time we saw him. It was empowering." (While I have written about not using the negative terms, in this case –– as long as it works, I say use whatever wording is best for you and your healing team.)

While focusing on belief, make time to examine your belief system. For example, are your beliefs truly your own or are they based on what others have told you? Did you grow up with people saying negative or positive things to you and about you? Which ones did you choose to believe?

What we believe and what we put out to the world are not necessarily the beliefs that are truly ours. If you grew up being told "you are ugly," "you won't succeed," etc., these beliefs may have taken seed and are now what you ***think*** you believe. Ask yourself if this is true or if you believe it because ***that's what you were always told***?

Work on changing your beliefs from those of others to those of your own voice and release the negative voices in your head. You may find by doing this, the healing process sets you on a more positive and confident path.

Healing Note

Believing and keeping positive is incredibly important throughout your healing journey and for life in general.

EXERCISES

1. Write down "I believe…" statements. Begin with what you believe because others have told you "this is truth." Then write statements of what you *truly* believe. Here is an example:

What I have been told by others.	What I truly believe about myself
Example: You are ugly.	Example: I am beautiful!
Example: You will never amount to anything.	Example: I am successful.

2. Repeat what you truly believe until you have forced out the beliefs that you were told.

3. Create affirmations around your beliefs.

```

```

4. Work with a coach or hypnotherapist or someone to help you release the old belief system and put into your mind the new one.

5. Find articles on changing your beliefs.

STEP FOUR: SELF–CARE!

Be your number one priority through self–care and self–love

"You can search throughout the entire universe for someone who is more deserving of your love and affection than you are yourself, and that person is not to be found anywhere. You yourself, as much as anybody in the entire universe deserve your love and affection."
Buddha

WE DO NOT HAVE THE ENERGY TO TAKE CARE OF OTHERS UNLESS WE TAKE CARE OF OURSELVES! So many people have said this phrase in one way or another. I truly believe it. I used to always be the person that gave to everyone else and didn't do enough for me. There have been a few times in my life that dis–ease has appeared to tell me to slow down and pay attention to what my body needs. I chose to listen to my body.

Learn to listen to your body. Take at least a moment every day to sit quietly and ask what your body needs. It tells you in so many ways what it needs. Take heed! Do the small things it asks of you before ***your body tells you that*** *you need to make a lot of changes and do it now*. Many times, a dis–ease comes into your life to push you to make changes.

Think about times you have become ill. What was going on in your life during the time prior to or during the illness? Did you say, "This is the worst possible time to become ill?" or "Why now?" Think back and meditate on the message(s) the illness sent you at those times, see if there are patterns and take time to figure out the message of the current illness. This is another good time to utilize your journal.

There is a lot of information out about healthy eating and self–care, but basically ***keep it simple***.

Feed yourself clean, organic healthy food. A great guideline is the yearly list of the Dirty Dozen put out by Environmental Working Group at ewg.org. (This a great site for information on chemicals in our food and environment.) This list is the list of foods that if purchased conventional and not organic contain the most chemicals. Eating organic of the following foods is highly suggested.

1. Strawberries
2. Spinach
3. Nectarines
4. Apples
5. Peaches
6. Celery
7. Grapes
8. Pears
9. Cherries

10. Tomatoes
11. Sweet bell peppers
12. Potatoes

The group also identifies the "Clean 15" or foods with the least likelihood to contain pesticide residue:

1. Sweet corn
2. Avocados
3. Pineapples
4. Cabbage
5. Onions
6. Frozen sweet peas
7. Papayas
8. Asparagus
9. Mangoes
10. Eggplant
11. Honeydew
12. Kiwifruit
13. Cantaloupe
14. Cauliflower
15. Grapefruit

Ways to keep it simple:
- Remove processed food and fast food from your daily eating.
- Exercise at least 30 minutes daily or whatever you are able to do. Even five minutes of exercise is better than nothing at all.
- Drink lots of water (see Healing Note)
- Get plenty of restful sleep. This is both during the

night and possibly throughout the day—if a nap is necessary, take it without guilt.

- Find ways to pamper yourself—see additional suggestions in the exercises below.
- Always keep your stress in line. Find ways to create calm instead of chaos. Lots of the exercises in this book will help you with this.

Healing Note

To determine the amount of recommended water, take your body weight and divide it by two. This equals the number of ounces per day that is correct for you. For instance, if you weigh 140 pounds, then you would want to drink 70 ounces or just under nine 8–ounce cups of water each day. It is also important to consider the amount of water you drink per hour. If you consistently drink more water per hour than recommended, you might overwork your kidneys and deplete your electrolytes and minerals.

I could go on and on about healthy eating and self-care. It really is simple once you make the choice to **prioritize yourself at the top of your list** instead of at the bottom or not even on your list of things to do. Again, if you say this will be hard, it will be. Pay attention to the words you use when you are planning on healing and taking care of yourself.

One of the top items for self-care to prioritize is managing your energy. You only have so much energy in a day, and each day will be different. Figure out how to best utilize your energy and do what you are able, then

ASK FOR HELP! This is something that can be a real challenge for many people, especially women. When you are healing, a lot of your energy will go towards the healing and we all have a lot of things to do during the day. Figure out what you are able to do without wearing yourself out, then ask for help with the rest of it. Friends and family don't know what you need until you tell them, so when they ask, don't hesitate and be specific. You can also check with your religious community to see if they have a caring community committee or something like this that helps with driving, meals, etc. There are many organizations that offer help with rides, free house cleaning, care taking, etc. Do your research or have someone help you do research.

Healing Note

*To be able to heal you need to come to the realization that you are not able to do everything because your energy is low and you need lots energy to heal. People truly do want to help and, unless you tell them what you really need, they have no idea. They may think it is a great idea to bring you a casserole for dinner made with noodles when you are not able to eat gluten. This is a waste of time for them and for you. Be proactive in telling people what you need and want! This is a very important step and **I know you can do it! Give it a try and find out how truly empowering and helpful it is!***

In my opinion, we have been conditioned to believe that asking for help is a weakness. I have found that ***asking for help is a strength***! I learned what my limits were and realized getting through the healing journey was not going to happen if I tried to do everything myself. I didn't have the energy to heal and handle all the everyday things.

Remember how good it makes you feel to help someone else when they really need you. Give others the gift to feel the same way when you ask them for help!

EXERCISES

1. Commit to a time for self–care each and every day!

2. Write yourself a love letter. Do this on some really beautiful stationary that makes you feel loved.

3. Create a self–care diary to set an intention of at least two things you can do today to take care of yourself. Write down what that is going to be and when you are going to do it.

4. Set a bedtime and go to bed at the same time each day in a very dark room with no electronics and no distractions.

5. Create daily affirmations around changing how you feel about yourself, focusing on what you believe and not what others told you were truth. Take some of the affirmations that call to you and create three that resonate with what you want to affirm for yourself. Write these down and post them wherever you will see them and say them during the day. If you Google "daily affirmations," you will find ways to receive daily affirmations in your email in box and you can also use these ideas to create your own affirmations.

6. Take a long bath using bath salts or Epsom salt. Be careful which ones you buy, though; soaking in chemicals is not a helpful way to heal. Look for ones that are chemical free, find all–natural homemade ones or make them yourself. (recipes can be found online). I personally love the bath salts from Little Moon Essentials.

Here is an affirmation I wrote and use at workshops: (This is also part of a meditation I have for free on my website at www.tirtzahsandor.com. Sign up for the Mindset for Healing Meditation and you also receive a bonus meditation that includes the following affirmation.)

Place your hand over your heart for a better heart connection– this is an affirmation/meditation for you to promise yourself that you will take time for self–care and to nurture yourself.

Take a deep breath

Repeat the following silently or out loud

I listen to my heart when I need to make a decision

I take time each day to do at least one thing to pamper myself

I feed my body healthy foods

I am mindful of my breathing

I laugh for the fun of laughing

I think positive thoughts

I am grateful for all the wonderful people in my life

I am grateful for all the wonderful things in my life

I create the life I desire

I give myself permission to surrender when and where I choose.

I give myself permission to nurture myself

I make time for all these things.

Send love and laughter to yourself

Send love and laughter to those you love

Send love and laughter to the world

Remember—You have to take care of yourself to be able to take care of others.

Take a deep breath

STEP FIVE: EMPOWERMENT!

Empower yourself and don't give into the fear

> *Technology has a shadow side. It accounts for real progress in medicine, but has also hurt it in many ways, making it more impersonal, expensive and dangerous. The false belief that a safety net of sophisticated drugs and machines stretches below us, permitting risky or lazy lifestyle choices, has undermined our spirit of self-reliance.*
> ***Andrew Weil, MD***

To empower yourself and set aside fear, you **have** to believe in yourself. Remember Step Three—Believe! Once you believe in yourself you will find that you know your body best. **Ask questions!** Don't just listen to the medical world because you have been taught they know what is best. Just like you, they know what they have been taught, and there is a wealth of other information on line and in pamphlets from organizations. Note: make sure you check the sources.

> *"Learn from yesterday, live for today, hope for tomorrow. The important thing is not to stop questioning."*
> **Albert Einstein**

DO NOT GIVE INTO THE FEAR by how some of the medical world may treat you.

In my opinion, many (not all) doctors, use the fear factor for you to listen to them. I found this when I went for a second opinion about the breast cancer diagnosis and found myself in an exam room sitting on a chair surrounded by a group of about eight doctors in their white coats, standing above me. They kept trying to tell me what to do and when I asked questions they reacted as if to say "how dare you question me?!" I knew then this was not the team for me. I knew my opinion about my treatment and my input would not be taken into consideration at any point during my treatment, so I chose to stay with my original team. I am grateful that I did.

Find a doctor or doctors who will work **with** you and respect your opinion. Also, remember to respect theirs so you can work together to heal.

Always take someone with you to appointments. When you are the one seeing the doctor(s), you may hear one word that throws you into other thoughts and you might miss the really important things the doctor says. Ask the person with you to take notes and then review the notes with them after the appointment. They most likely will hear something you did not. *If you have additional questions, follow up with the doctor and ask for clarification.*

In my opinion, when you are on a healing journey—your questions are the ***most*** important factor. **ASK THEM**! No question is "dumb" or "stupid." Questions are how you educate and empower yourself to make the decisions that are right for you.

Asking for additional time to do research before allowing any doctor to do a procedure can also be beneficial. You are probably in an emotional state over what they have told you. Don't allow anyone to push you into something you don't feel is right.

Do your research. If you are not a good researcher, ask a friend (or many friends) to help you get the best information and be mindful of your information sources. Remember that not everything on the internet is true; make sure you are looking at or speaking to trusted sources. I was given "trusted resources" in informational pamphlets from the hospital. I was told not to look at any other sources. I researched the ones I was given by the medical team and then also found my own. While I found that their sources agreed with the information they were handing out or telling me, I would still encourage you to look at everything; medical, alternative, complementary, eastern medicine, ayurvedic medicine, energy healing, supplements, etc. Take whatever resonates with you and ask questions, ask for referrals from friends, and speak to others that have used the treatments. Empower yourself to move forward with what is best for you!

When you come across information you think will benefit you, discuss it with your doctor(s). If you find something that works for you, share with your doctor(s). It may not only help you, but could potentially help others too!

Healing Note

*FOLLOW YOUR GUT! If you get a feeling in your stomach or your stomach is in knots, it most likely means what is being told to you is not right for you. If you feel relaxed and calm about the information, then go with it. **Believe in yourself and what your intuition is telling you. This is how you empower yourself!!***

EXERCISES

1. Think about what you want in your doctors.

2. Visualize the right doctors being there for you.

3. Write down how you want to see the treatment going after you have done your research.

4. Breathe into any fear you may be experiencing. Spend time with the fear. Allow it to help you figure out why it is there. Ask it to explain. Figure out where in your body the fear is located and breathe it out.

5. Write down all your questions for your doctors and take them with you to each appointment. Keeping a notebook only for your medical information will be very helpful in keeping track of all the information during your healing journey.

STEP SIX: DIRECTION

Follow your own path

> *"Everyone has choices to make; no one has the right to take those choices away from us. Not even out of love."*
> **Cassandra Clare, City of Ashes**

What choices are you going to make to follow your own path? What did you find in your research that needs more looking into? What do you believe is the right path for you to take? These are all questions you need to ask yourself and to ask your doctor.

Speak with your doctor(s) about what you feel is best and if they are not onboard, you may want to find a new doctor(s). If you choose to go against what you feel is right and choose to only follow the medical path, you *may* have lifelong regrets (see healing note above about following your intuition or gut). If you choose to just go down the medical path, that is fine, just be aware there are other ways of treating dis–eases creating healing, and you want to choose what is best for you.

Healing Note

*Once you have done your research, listen to your body and your intuition and do what is best for you. **Only you** can decide what is really the best path for your personal healing journey.*

During two of my healing journeys, (sick building syndrome and breast cancer), I made choices other people disagreed with. I chose to stand by my convictions and did what I felt was right for me. I truly believe this is part of the reason I am here to write this book and share with the world that there is more than one way to help people heal.

EXERCISES

1. Read books that call to you to help you heal. I would look up whatever sounded good to me, then check them out from the library. If they really resonated, I purchased them. (See book list on the Resource page.)

2. Find complementary, integrative, alternative, or other non–medical treatments. There are many out there. The following are some that kept me going and helped me heal and many of these I continue to incorporate into my lifestyle practice.

   - Hypnotherapy
   - Acupuncture
   - Reiki
   - Healing Touch
   - Chakra balancing
   - Massage
   - Bio–feedback
   - Shamans
   - Herbalists
   - Ayurveda Medicine
   - Chinese Medicine
   - Supplements

   There are many names for "energy healing." Ask

around to find the wonderful healers in your area. Set an intention to find the right ones for you. (I have provided a list on the Resource Page of the healers I used in Columbus, Ohio.)

STEP SEVEN: POSITIVITY

Create a positive mindset

> *"Create a positive attitude to change any situation.*
> *Although it may be a challenge, it is worth the effort."*
> **Tirtzah Sandor**

Being positive can be very challenging at times, but you **CAN** do it. There is so much research on the power of positive thinking and evidence shows how much of a difference it can make.

An article in the Harvard Gazette entitled "The Power of Positive Thinking" states, "Having an optimistic outlook on life — a general expectation that good things will happen — may help people live longer, according to a new study from the Harvard T.H. Chan School of Public Health. The study found that women who were optimistic had a significantly reduced risk of dying from several major causes of death — including cancer, heart disease, stroke, respiratory disease, and infection — over an eight–year period, compared with women who were less optimistic."[8]

"I think of positive emotions as nutrients. In the same way that we need to eat a variety of fruits and vegetables to be healthy, we need a variety of positive emotions in our daily experience to help us become more resourceful versions of ourselves,' says Professor Barbara Frederickson, University of North Carolina in an article entitled: Scientific evidence points to important of positive thinking." [9]

Positive thoughts actually change your physiology. They release endorphins into your body and push out cortisol. This process lowers your stress level creating a double benefit of less stress and more healing.

Part of creating a positive mindset is using positive words. As I pointed out in the beginning, if you are fighting, battling, conquering or being a warrior, you are in effect defeating the purpose of healing.

Use words like:
- Strong
- Strength
- Supported
- Loved
- Blessed
- Abundant
- Believe
- Calm
- Creative
- Easy

Take "can't" and "try" out of your vocabulary.
- Can't actually means **cannot but,** as in "I have no alternative but to"
- Try means to make an attempt or effort; strive;

an effort to accomplish something; an attempt

Another word to take out of your vocabulary is the word hard. What do you think of when something is hard. I think of a brick wall. Something that cannot be moved. I prefer the word challenge because a challenge can be overcome.

When you use negative words, you most likely won't move forward. Stop blocking yourself with negativity and be positive. Say *"I can"* and **take action. BE STRONG! BE BOLD! Accomplish what you want to do instead of just trying.**

Healing Note

Think about the words you choose to use and think. Negative words and thoughts beget negative actions; positive words and thoughts beget positive actions.

Using negative words puts your body in a state of negativity and stress: two conditions that are not good for your body any time and **especially** when you are on a healing journey. Words and thoughts make a difference. (This is true for life in general.)

In Step One I presented an exercise to keep a gratitude journal. Being grateful is another way to switch the mind and body from a negative state to a positive state. More and more research is being done on gratitude and how it can help. In June 2017, the University of Minnesota asked people using Caringbridge to participate in a gratitude study. They sent out an initial survey at the beginning then asked participants to write three things they were grateful for at the end of the day. At the end of each week, they asked participants to review their gratitude journals to see if there were any patterns and what had changed, then sent the same survey to see how/if the questions were answered differently at the end. I chose to participate, because I believe gratitude is one of the best ways to change your mindset. When I am not able to fall asleep at night, because I have monkey brain (my brain never stops and all kinds of thoughts are constantly going through my head), I make myself concentrate on everything I am grateful for and am able to fall asleep. I also do this during the day when I begin to feel negative. Practicing gratitude is another way to change your physiology and change to a positive mindset.

Each of us has so many things to be grateful for, even during the darkest times.

Two examples of articles on research now being conducted on the effects of positive thinking and health are below. I took a small sampling of each article and have supplied the url if you choose to read more.

In the article titled "The Science of Positive Thinking," Dr. Joseph Mercola states: "Can your mind heal your body? It may sound far–fetched that the power of your thoughts and emotions could exert physical, biological changes, but there are countless examples, both scientific and anecdotal, showing this possibility is very real." [10]

In an article in Scientific American titled: The Science of Healing by Gareth Cook, interviewing Jo Marchant, PhD, is an award–winning science journalist and author of Cure: A Journey into the Science of Mind over Body. Jo Marchant states: "There are now several lines of research suggesting that our mental perception of the world constantly informs and guides our immune system in a way that makes us better able to respond to future threats. That was a sort of 'aha' moment for me — where the idea of an entwined mind and body suddenly made more scientific sense than an ephemeral consciousness that's somehow separated from our physical selves." [11]

I am personally grateful that the science behind the mind–body–spirit connection is finally catching up with what much of the world has known for a very long time!

"Once you replace negative thoughts with positive ones, you'll start having positive results."
Willie Nelson

"You can do everything you can to try to stop bad things from happening to you, but eventually things will happen, so the best prevention is a positive attitude."
Marie Osmond

EXERCISES

1. Change negative thoughts and speech into positive thoughts and speech.

Worksheet to Change Negative Thoughts and Speech into Positive Thoughts and Speech	
Write down the negative thought you say or think. Example: I really screwed up.	Turn the negative into a positive statement. Example: I made a mistake and will make changes next time.
Negative	Positive

2. Compare feelings on negative and positive thoughts and word.

Comparing Feelings on Negative and Positive Thoughts and Words

My negative thoughts and negative sayings (words). (Things I say to myself):

_____

_____

_____

_____

How do I feel now after writing them all down?

_____

_____

_____

_____

My positive thoughts and positive sayings (words):

_____

_____

_____

_____

How do I feel now?

_____

_____

_____

_____

Take time to review what you wrote and revisit this worksheet whenever you need to. Feel free to add to it as you move through the journey.

3. Find a great counselor or coach to work with to help you view the "negative" events in your life to seeing them from a positive perspective.

4. Attend a mindfulness class to help you concentrate on being more positive in your life.

5. Surround yourself with positive people. Sometimes people in our life tend to be very negative and bring us down. Look at who you hang around with and make a choice to believe in yourself and release the negative people in your life.

POSITIVE	NEGATIVE

STEP EIGHT: FORGIVENESS

Forgive yourself, then forgive others

> *"Forgiveness is for yourself because it frees you. It lets you out of that prison you put yourself in."*
> **Louise L. Hay**
>
> *"The weak can never forgive. Forgiveness is the attribute of the strong."*
> ***Mahatma Gandhi***
>
> *"Forgiveness says you are given another chance to make a new beginning."*
> ***Desmond Tutu***
>
> *"Holding onto resentment is like drinking poison and expecting the other person to die"*
> ***Famous quote***

Anger caused by the past or other emotions that you have not dealt with may be a part of the cause of the disease. Forgiving others and letting go of the past allows you to move forward and gives you a new mindset for healing and new perspective on life.

> *"For every minute you remain angry, you give up sixty seconds of peace of mind."*
> **Ralph Waldo Emerson**

The first step in forgiving is to take responsibility for your actions and your choices of how you reacted in the heat of the situation.

I didn't have the best relationship with my family from a very early age. I carried a lot of anger a good portion of my life. The more I read and studied the more I realized how this anger and negativity was affecting not only me and my health but all of my relationships.

When I chose to forgive myself for allowing their words and actions to affect me so much and realized they did the best they could with what they knew and believed from their own experiences, I began to heal.

This helped some relationships, but there were others where it didn't matter what I said or did to reach out. For those, I had to learn to let go, move on, and understand they were making the best choice for them and nothing was going to change this *for them*. It was *their* issue to deal with, *not mine*. I chose to let go and move on.

Forgiving others is the easier part of this equation, whereas forgiving yourself can be one of the biggest challenges we each face. It opens vulnerabilities you may not even realize you have. You may be able to work through this process alone, but I highly recommend working with a coach or counselor to move through it.

As you work through forgiveness, you may discover

that part of the dis-ease you have been diagnosed with might be the result of beliefs you have allowed others to instill in you, potentially creating the anger and pain you possibly carry inside as dis-ease.

If you choose to reach out to someone and ask for forgiveness, you may find they will not remember the incident but rather this was something you blew up in your mind. While it had a major effect on you, the other person may have never noticed the incident or words or whatever you are asking forgiveness for. If they do remember and your apology touches them, you will not only be helping yourself heal, you may be helping them heal also.

Healing Note

Forgiving yourself and forgiving others is one of the key components to healing.

EXERCISES

1. Imagine yourself as someone you want to forgive and ask yourself questions. Respond from where you believe their perspective is as best as you are able. This may help you see things from their point of view and change how you see the situation.

2. Write notes forgiving the person (or yourself) which you can send to them, or you can burn, tear up, delete, etc. and simply send the forgiveness out to the universe, god, or wherever you imagine it going.

3. Reach out to someone you wish to forgive and say you are sorry.

4. Create forgiveness affirmations.

5. Write down everything you feel was done against you and then write something positive that came out of the experience. (Example: I grew up in a home where I was never good enough. This experience led me to be strong and gave me the conviction to succeed.)

6. Create gratitude around what each person or situation has brought to you, even the negative ones.

7. A simple ancient mantra from Hawaii is the Ho'opopono which means "to make right". It is a mantra to send out energy for creating forgiveness to the person you are sending this to and for them to forgive you.

    Recite:
    I love you
    I'm sorry
    Please forgive me
    Thank you

The Process of Ho'oponopono [12]

1. Bring to mind anyone with whom you do not feel total alignment or support, etc.

2. In your mind's eye, construct a small stage below you

3. Imagine an infinite source of love and healing flowing from a source above the top of your head (from your Higher Self), and open up the top of your head, and let the source of love and healing flow down inside your body, fill up the body, and overflow out your heart to heal up the person on the stage. Be sure it is all right for you to heal the person and that they accept the healing.

4. When the healing is complete, have a discussion with the person and forgive them, and have them forgive you.

5. Next, let go of the person, and see them floating away. As they do, cut the aka cord that connects the two of you (if appropriate). If you are healing in a current primary relationship, then assimilate the person inside you.

6. Do this with every person in your life with whom you are incomplete, or not aligned.

The final test is, can you see the person or think of them without feeling any negative emotions. If you do feel negative emotions when you do, then do the process again.

STEP NINE: ENJOYMENT!

Laugh and smile

> *"There is no laughter in the medicine; but there is a lot of medicine in the laughter."*
> **Madan Kataria**
>
> *"Laughter is an instant vacation."*
> **Milton Berle**
>
> *"Laughter is a powerful way to tap positive emotions."*
> **Norman Cousins**

Laughter truly is the best medicine. Norman Cousins was able to cure himself of the diagnosis of ankylosing spondylitis, a degenerative disease of the connective tissue the doctors said he would never recover from. He said, "Ten minutes of genuine belly laughter had an anesthetic effect and would give me at least two hours of pain–free sleep."

It has been proven scientifically that laughter is a great way to start the day. It helps you focus and be more productive. It is simple and free. It helps build relationships and everyone can do it. Below are some additional health benefits of laughter:

- Boosts the immune system
- Reduces stress
- Reduces blood pressure
- Lifts mild depression
- Promotes relaxation
- Expands lung capacity
- Increases oxygen to the lungs
- Exercises abdomen and diaphragm
- Increases circulation
- Helps memory loss by stopping neuron damage because you are reducing the cortisol level in your body

During my healing journey when I felt myself sinking into depression, I would watch something funny and my spirits would lift. I watched a TV show or comedy movie or got on the computer and watched silly YouTube videos (cat videos are my favorite). The more I laughed, the better I felt.

Healing Note

Laughter isn't just for healing.
Give yourself permission to laugh a lot!

Another way to lift your spirits is by smiling. When I went to the chemotherapy sessions, I was known as the "smiley face lady" for two reasons: I always went in with a smile on my face, and I gave out smiley face stickers and magnets to help brighten everyone's day. It was great therapy for me and it made the day a little brighter for the people who worked at the facility and those coming in for treatments.

As a Certified Laughter Yoga Leader, I understand the power of laughter. I once did a session at a nursing home. Almost everyone was in a wheelchair. By the end of the session everyone was smiling and some were laughing. The nurses were amazed by the changes. Some of the attendees had not smiled or laughed for a very long time.

Healing Note

Fake it until you are actually smiling and/or laughing. (Fake laughter gives you the same benefits as real laughter except for the deep belly laughter, which also helps the core so that is the best.)

EXERCISES

1. Find a Laughter Yoga circle—most are free.

2. Laughter Yoga Website: https://laughteryoga.org/

3. Call or visit with a friend and laugh about anything.

4. Smile at everyone even when you don't feel like smiling!

5. Just Laugh!

6. Remember to laugh at yourself and not take yourself so seriously!

STEP TEN:
LIVE!

Do whatever you are able to do to enjoy life during and after the healing journey

> *"Even if you have a terminal dis–ease, you don't have to sit down and mope. Enjoy life and challenge the illness that you have."*
> **Nelson Mandela**

In *The Power of Now*, a book about living in the present moment, Eckhart Tolle says "Accessing the deepest self, the true self, can be learned, by freeing ourselves from the conflicting, unreasonable demands of the mind and living present, fully, and intensely, in the Now." He speaks about how we create our own pain and if we find ways to live in the present, we can create a pain–free existence.

When you stop worrying about the future and put your attention on what is going on in the present moment, take time to enjoy and live it to the fullest, your life becomes richer and your healing journey is enhanced.

> *"Give up waiting as a state of mind. When you catch yourself slipping into the waiting, snap out of it. Come in the present moment. Just be, and enjoy being. If you are present, there is never any need for you to wait for anything."*
> **Eckhart Tolle**

Stop waiting for the right time to savor life. Ask yourself: "how can I fully live today?" Embrace and be grateful for a new day and the new opportunities it brings. Ask yourself:

- How am I going to take a step forward with what I have learned so that I am able to do today what I want to do?
- What is my intention for this new day?
- What can I use from the exercises I have done to move myself forward?
- What resonates with me?
- What do I have the energy to do today?
- How am I going to take care of myself?
- What movements am I going to do?
- What answers came to you from asking yourself these questions? Take a moment and write them down so you don't forget and have the answers return to later.

Healing Note

Doing something—no matter how small, takes you to a different environment—even if it is just for a short period of time.

Move

One of the best things you can do to live is to keep moving, however much you are able. During my breast cancer healing journey, even on the days I had chemotherapy, I had my husband "walk" me. We used this phrase because some days I didn't have the energy to walk on my own. He had to really support me. Some days he walked me a short distance, some days I was able to go further. Each day I did it and was grateful for whatever distance I was able to walk, even on the days I was not able to do as much as the day before. Our bodies are meant to move and when we don't, they begin to break down. Make sure you do some type of movement each day.

If you are able, attend any type of movement class. If you are not able to attend a class, consider finding classes on tv or the internet to move to. Try something new. If you have never tried yoga, Tai Chi, or QiGong, now would be a good time to try. All have a mindfulness element to them that also helps with focusing and healing. Remember: any movement is better than nothing at all!

Many places, especially those associated with cancer treatments offer FREE classes. Check with local dis–ease associations to see what they have to offer.

Breathe

One of the best things you can do for yourself to live is to learn to breath properly to help you heal and to have more energy. Dr. Andrew Weil said, *"If I had to limit my advice on healthier living to just one tip—it would be simply to learn to breathe correctly."*

Breath is life; the more you are conscious of your breathing, the better you will feel. (See Exercise #1 on how to breath.)

Plan

Another way to live is to plan for the future. This gives you something to focus on and move forward to.

Make a bucket list of things you want to do and **start doing them**. What is on your list that you can do right now?

Learn

Is there a class you have always wanted to take? With online classes, you can potentially find whatever piques your interest and do it at home, or get out and be among other people by taking a class locally.

Travel

As I spoke about earlier in the book, during my healing journey I traveled. It was challenging at times, but it was very important for me to keep up my positive mindset for healing. I had to do a lot of resting during the travel, and that was ok. I got to be away from home, in different environments, and I was with positive people who helped make sure I was not overdoing it. It zapped my energy and took me a lot of time to recover after, but it was worth every minute!

Help Others

Doing something good for others lifts your spirits. It may be something small, such as a phone call. Figure out your limits and take a moment to do something for someone else.

What is it that makes you feel alive? Whatever it is, do it! How do you plan on challenging the dis–ease that you have? How will you choose to live?

EXERCISES

1. Breathe! Teach yourself to breathe from your belly. When you breathe in, use your diaphragm and your belly should rise. When you breathe out, your belly should fall. To practice, lay on your back and put a small magazine on your belly and make the magazine rise and fall.

2. Do any kind of movement even if it is just a little, exercise as much as you are able. Do as little or as much as you can. Know that each day your energy level will be different and that is ok.

3. Learn to go with the flow and enjoy!!!

4. Travel if you are able. Making plans and traveling is a great way to keep a positive attitude. Remember, when you travel, your energy level may be lower than you would like. Make sure you care for yourself during the time you are gone from your home.

5. Watch a travel video if you are not able to travel. At least this way you are able to visualize traveling somewhere.

6. Read. Find books that are fun to read or that take you

to places you want to go. You can read the actual book or listen to it with Audible or other online resources.

7. Create a morning ritual to get your day started. My ritual is that I meditate, journal, then eat breakfast. I do the things I don't really like to do or the thing that is most important first. Then I move onto the rest of my day with gratitude that I completed the one thing that needed to get done.

8. Do whatever lights you up!

SUGGESTIONS FOR CELEBRATIONS

Research shows that taking moments to pause, be mindful and celebrate boosts your well–being. Taking time to savor all the positive changes or events in your life, you change the negative energy to positive and this helps you build resilience. With this resilience, you can more easily manage challenges that may otherwise cause stress in your life.

When we have a celebration to look forward to, we are more optimistic. The celebration does not have to be anything big, just something you really enjoy.

> *"Celebrate all of your accomplishments, especially the small ones, they may be the most important accomplishments."*
> **Tirtzah Sandor**

Be creative and find celebrations that really resonate with you and with what you have accomplished.

Celebrate your accomplishments through your mindset for healing journey and remember to celebrate other wonderful events in your life!

The following are some celebration suggestions:

1. Go out with friend(s)

2. Share your choice or choices or accomplishment(s) with friend(s)

3. Buy yourself something you have always wanted

4. Enjoy a healthy treat

5. Get a makeover to enhance your beautiful self

6. Do something special with your partner

7. Buy yourself something connected with your spirituality

8. Take a deep breath

9. Feel gratitude

10. Cheer for yourself

11. Dance

12. Treat yourself to a day of rest and relaxation

13. Connect with someone you've been thinking about and haven't spoken to in a while or years

14. Buy yourself flowers

15. Buy someone else flowers

16. Plan a trip

17. Go for a nature walk

18. Go on a cultural outing: symphony, play, concert, dance performance, museum etc.

19. Give a gift to someone to say thank you

20. Make a donation in your honor or in someone else's honor or memory

21. Take a bath

22. Pick a theme song for your life and listen to it often

CONCLUSION

In my opinion, life is meant to be lived and enjoyed no matter your circumstances, healthy or not so healthy. By adopting this attitude and adjusting to a mindset for healing, and seeing healing from a new perspective, especially during a challenging illness, you will live life to the fullest in every moment.

I did it and I know you can too!

By taking the steps in this book, along with working with your doctors and healers, I believe your healing journey will be easier and more profound.

I am sending healing energy to you to help release whatever dis–ease you have, whatever you need to heal from and to help you on your healing journey.

May your days be filled with love, laughter, joy, abundance, forgiveness, and healing.

RESOURCES

More resources can be found at www.mindsetforhealing.com or https://www.tirtzahsandor.com/ Both links take you to tirtzahsandor.com.

I have a free Mindset for Healing Meditation and a bonus meditation on my site.

Links to Articles

https://www.ncbi.nlm.nih.gov/pmc/articles/PMC4623985/
http://www.breastcancer.org/treatment/comp_med
https://www.drweil.com/health–wellness/balanced–living/meet–dr–weil/what–is–integrative–medicine/

Website Links for Sharing Your Journey

https://www.caringbridge.org
https://posthope.org/
http://lotsahelpinghands.com/
http://www.giveforward.com/

Website Links for Grounding Mats

Note: I have not purchased any of these products so this is not an endorsement; just information.

https://www.earthing.com

http://products.mercola.com/earthing-mat/
Note: Dr. Mercola has a video on this site about grounding.

https://www.amazon.com/dp/B003RLOBOK

All Natural Products I Have Used and Love

Little Moon Essentials: Bath salts, natural vapor rub https://littlemoonessentials.com/

Infuse Organics: https://www.infuseorganics.com/

Suggested Reading

The Flow Method—Tara Meyer-Robinson
The Biology of Belief—Bruce H. Lipton, PhD
Anatomy of an Illness—Norman Cousins
You Can Heal Your Life—Louise L. Hay
The Last Best Cure—Donna Jackson Nakazawa
The Four Levels of Healing—Shakti Gawain
Love, Medicine and Miracles—by Bernie Siegel, MD
Anatomy of the Spirit—Caroline Myss
The Way of the Peaceful Warrior—Dan Millman

About the Author

Tirtzah Sandor and her husband, Rick, were living the life they had been working towards for years. Rick had landed his dream job and Tirtzah was in business for herself as a certified health and wellness coach.

The universe had different plans.

In January of 2016, right before her 60th birthday, Tirtzah was diagnosed with breast cancer. She immediately stepped aside from her business and put all her energy into healing herself and releasing the cancer.

Tirtzah started keeping a daily journal chronicling her journey. She posted often on Caringbridge.org to keep family and friends informed.

"People kept telling me that I needed to write my story," said Tirtzah. She agreed and began a book about her experiences.

This isn't that book...

"As I was writing I realized that what was getting me through and allowing me to release the cancer was the mindset that I used. My healing mindset. So, I decided to set that first book aside. The most important thing became doing whatever I could to help other people."

Tirtzah made the choice to not let the cancer or any past healing journeys define her. She learned that many past issues that needed to be released likely brought on the dis-ease. "There was a lot of forgiveness needed–both toward myself and towards other people."

The mindset for healing wasn't new to the author, who grew up in a very negative, dysfunctional environment. "All my life I've been working on changing my mindset, attitude and words and helping others do the same," she said.

How did that translate into releasing the cancer? "I did what I've always done, but much more intensively and mindfully."

She also became acutely aware of her environment–making sure that everyone she came into contact with did the same. Loved ones were asked to maintain their own healing mindset towards Tirtzah's illness even when they were not with her.

"I didn't want to go down that path of 'poor me.' "

With the assistance of family, friends, and a whole team of practitioners from all walks of medicine and healing modalities. "I asked the universe to bring me what and who I needed."

Did it ever! From medical specialists to shamans,

Tirtzah listened to her inner wisdom and met and worked with an amazing community of healers in her journey.

Tirtzah Sandor is an empath and intuitive that uses her gifts as a Certified Holistic Health and Wellness Coach specializing in mindset for healing. She has completed Reiki Level 2. She lives in Columbus, Ohio with her husband. They have one adult daughter. Tirtzah loves to travel, sew, crochet, volunteer, and laugh.

Other Publishings

April 2015—Central Ohio Natural Awakenings Magazine—April is Stress Management Month

April 2015—Gahanna Chamber of Commerce Business to Business Newsletter—April is Stress Management Month

Nov. 16, 2013 Trenton Ohio Newspaper The Observer—Health Revolutions

National Website for The Transition Network—The Last Third of My life—June 16, 2017

Notes

1   National Center for Biotechnology Information.

2   Healthcare and treatment practices, including traditional Chinese medicine, chiropractic, folk medicine, and naturopathy, that minimize or eschew the use of surgery and drugs. DICTIONARY.COM

Complementary medicine embraces "a wide range of treatments for medical conditions that people use instead of or in addition to ordinary medicine: Acupuncture, reflexology, and homeopathy are all forms of complementary medicine." CAMBRIDGE DICTIONARY.COM

"Integrative Medicine (IM) is healing–oriented medicine that takes account of the whole person, including all aspects of lifestyle. It emphasizes the therapeutic relationship between practitioner and patient, is informed by evidence, and makes use of all appropriate therapies." University of Arizona Center for Integrative Medicine and Ayurvedic Medicine

"Ayurvedic medicine is a system of healing that originated in ancient India. In Sanskrit, ayur means life or living, and veda means knowledge, so Ayurveda has been defined as the 'knowledge of living' or the 'science of longevity.' Ayurvedic medicine utilizes diet, detoxification and purification techniques, herbal and mineral remedies, yoga, breathing exercises, meditation, and massage therapy as holistic healing methods. Ayurvedic medicine is widely practiced in modern India and has been steadily gaining followers in the West." The Free Dictionary.com Medical Dictionary

3   Webster Dictionary

4   Dr. Candace Pert (1946–2013) has been called "The Mother of Psychoneuroimmunology", and "The Goddess of Neuroscience" by her many fans. To her colleagues she was an internationally recognized neuroscientist and pharmacologist who published over 250 research articles and was a significant contributor to the emergence of Mind–Body Medicine as an area of legitimate scientific research in the 1980's.

5   A port is a small disc made of plastic or metal about the size of a quarter that sits just under the skin. A soft thin tube called a catheter connects the port to a large vein. Your chemotherapy medicines are given through a special needle that fits right into the port. You also can have blood drawn through the port. For more information, see "How Is Chemotherapy Given When Treating Breast Cancer?", www.breastcancer.org/treatment/chemotherapy/pro cess/how.

6   See http://www.nationalgeographic.com/magazine/2016 /12/healing–science–belief–placebo/

7   See http://articles.mercola.com/sites/articles/archive/20 15/03/05/placebo–effect–healing–recovery.aspx

8   See http://news.harvard.edu/gazette/story/2016/12/opt istic–women–live–longer–are–healthier/

9   See
     http://www.abc.net.au/radionational/programs/allin
     themind/the–scientific–evidence–for–positive–
     thinking/6553614

10   See
     http://articles.mercola.com/sites/articles/archive/20
     16/02/04/healing–thoughts.aspx

11   See https://www.scientificamerican.com/article/the–
     science–of–healing–thoughts/

12   http://www.ancienthuna.com/ho–oponopono.htm
     This article tells a lot more about the practice.

Made in the USA
Columbia, SC
23 October 2018